C000179435

BIRMINGHAM: MORE OF THE FIFTIES

Alton & Jo Douglas

Dale End/Moor Street, 1958.

© 2009 Alton and Jo Douglas
ISBN 978-1-85858-451-5
Published by Brewin Books Ltd., Doric House, 56 Alcester Road, Studley, Warwickshire B80 7LG.
Printed by Warwick Printing Co. Ltd., Caswell Road, Leamington Spa CV31 2QD.
Layout by Alton and Jo Douglas
All Rights Reserved

Gaskell & Chambers Ltd., (engineers), Dale End/Masshouse Lane, April 1958.

Front Cover: Corporation Street/Stephenson Place, 5th May 1955.

C o n t e n t s

BREWIN BOOKS LTD

Doric House, 56 Alcester Road,
Studley, Warwickshire B80 7LG

Tel: 01527 854228 Fax: 01527 852746

Vat Registration No. 705 0077 73

Dear Nostalgic,

I know, I know, I can't believe it either – it's half a century since the fifties came to an end! Now the decade has really become part of our history. To celebrate we've prepared a veritable feast for you. With a starter consisting of evocative old advertisements and posters; a main course of the street scenes you all love and as a sweet, a liberal helping of faces, some famous and some not so famous, it's time to indulge yourself. So, pour yourself a cup of coffee and prepare to wallow in a scrumptious collection of tasty memorabilia.

Incidentally, just to dispel any doubts you may have (after all this is our fourth book on the fifties) we work flat out to ensure that all the ingredients in our offerings are fresh i.e. none of them have ever been on our menu before. That means you're getting well over 300 items at a mouth-watering price. Anyway, I think that's enough references to food, you must be hungry by now!

Oh, just one more thing. I forgot to mention the appetiser – the cover pictures – the front has a super shot of New Street, from Stephenson Place to The Times building and on the back, the much-loved Aston Hippodrome. Wow! Pass the Alka Seltzer!

Yours, in friendship,

Stratford Road, Sparkhill, 16th April 1956.

1950

Preparing the evening meal, Grand Hotel, Colmore Row, 1950.
The hotel, which opened in 1875, finally closed in 2004, when
it was granted Grade 2 Listed status.

British film star, Valerie Hobson, is greeted by
Odeon manager, Mr E D Hainge, Snow Hill
Station, January 1950. She was on a promotion
tour for her film, " The Rocking
Horse Winner".

Colmore Row, c 1950. The Grand Hotel can be seen, on the left, immediately past Church Street.

Navigation Street, c 1950.

Martineau Street, from Corporation Street, 1950.

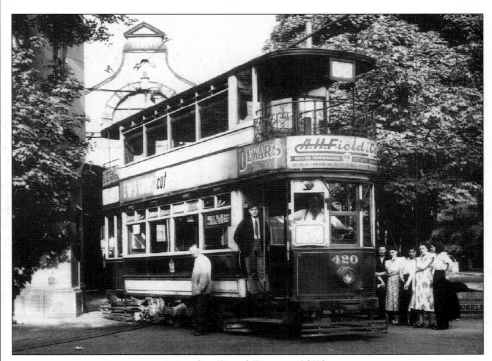

Moseley Road Depot, 1950.

Tilting test at Tyburn Road Works,
Erdington, c 1950

Bus washing machine, Yardley Wood Garage,
1950.

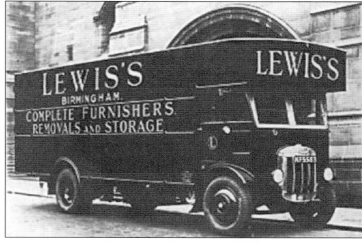

Lewis's delivery van, 1950

Kings Norton Youth Fellowship on holiday at Bembridge, Isle of Wight, Summer 1950.

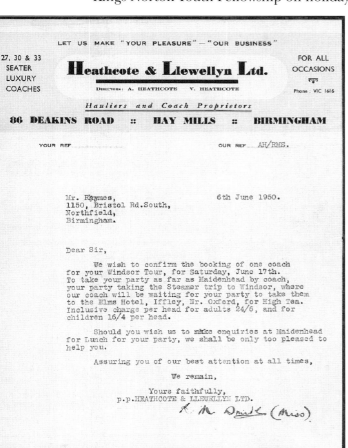

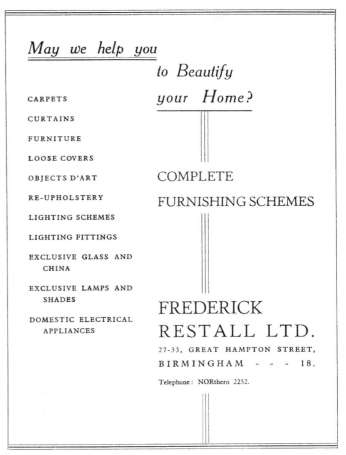

Members of Hall Green Little Theatre set about
building their own theatre, Summer 1950.

A policeman keeps a watchful eye
on street traders, Bull Ring, 1950.

The Kings Norton Cinema, 1950.

Bolton Road, Small Heath, 1950.

New Street, looking towards Bennetts Hill, 1950.

Jean Mason and Len Russell
rehearsing for a gig at the
Rendezvous Ballroom (The Lyon
Hall), Aston, with the Ray Fenton
Sextet, 1950

The lounge, Turkish Baths, Kent Street, 1950.

The Springfield cinema, Stratford Road, Sparkhill, 1950.

1951

Lewis's Players at Birmingham and Midland Institute, on 25th-26th January, are giving the first amateur production of *Duet For Two Hands*. This company was formed in 1945, and is an active example of a business house dramatic society.

Alcester Road South, Kings Heath, c 1951.

Lifford Lock, Kings Norton, 1951.

Lifford Reservoir, with Brandwood Park Road (top right) Kings Norton, 1951.

The Lord Mayor, Ald. Alfred Paddon Smith, with the French delegation,
after a wreath-laying ceremony at the Hall of Memory, 1st May 1951.

The salute from the Red Cross, following a service at St Philip's, taken by the Lord Mayor,
Ald. Ralph Yates, Colmore Row, 24th June 1951.

Enjoying the sun, with Baskerville House on the left and the Hall of Memory seen in all it's splendour, Summer 1951

Equestrian statue of King George I, outside
The Barber Institute of Fine Arts,
Birmingham University, 1951

Smith's Imperial Coaches garage, Stratford Road,
Sparkhill, 1951.

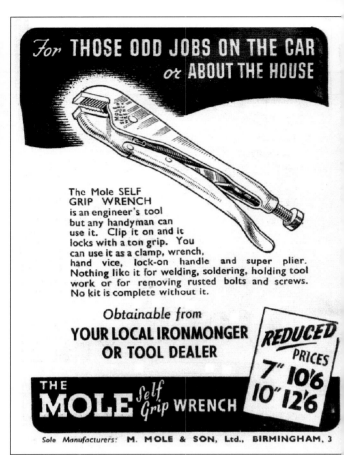

Demolition work on the site of the once-proud Empire Theatre, Hurst Steet/Smallbrook Street, 1951.

A blow from a sledgehammer fails to destroy the concrete slab on his chest and even more importantly, strongman, Tralavia himself! Bull Ring, 1951

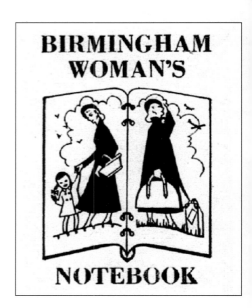

BIRMINGHAM WOMAN'S NOTEBOOK

Father Christmas arrives at Lewis's, 3rd November 1951.

One of the hit films of the year was "Fort Worth", starring Randolph Scott, 1951.

Fifteen tired film stars left New Street station to-day en route for Newcastle where the second replica Royal Film Performance takes place to-night.

This is the third major film occasion to which they have lent glitter in four days, and their work of rehearsal for the London event began last week.

The reception given to them by Birmingham last night surprised them all. Several thousand people thronged New Street to watch their arrival for the first replica Royal film show the city has had.

Most of the 50 police, mounted and on foot, were on continuous duty near the Odeon Theatre all evening as a large proportion of the young star-worshippers waited outside throughout the performance.

After braving the arc lights and the microphone at the entrance, the British and American actors and actresses began their five-hour task entertaining and "being met" at the reception given by The Birmingham Post and Mail, Ltd., rehearsing behind screens in the restaurant, appearing on the stage, and then attending a ball at the Grand Hotel.

Their stage appearance followed the showing of the Ealing Studios film, "Where No Vultures Fly," and a variety programme which included Terry-Thomas, Richard Murdoch and Kenneth Horne, with Geraldo and his orchestra.

"No Vultures" is the finest film of wild life one could wish to see. Hollywood may send gigantic caterpillar safari across the continent, but the result too often suggest that the pictures, beautiful in themselves, are of animals who have been dropped back into their natural habitat for a holiday from Whipsnade.

Living Colour

Further, shots which might have had reality are spoiled because we feel they were reached with a telescopic lens.

Here, director Harry Watt, associate producer Leslie Norman and camera units under Geoffrey Unsworth have got right up to their subject. Scrub and plain are tremulous with living colour.

The oft-recorded beauty of fleeting giraffe who seem to float along in slow motion, the grace of springing deer, the gentle majesty of lions lying in the shade, the conscientious elephants washing behind their frond-like ears—all are here more fresh and personal to the beholder.

In vivid close-ups the animals seem to move out of the screen into the cinema. At least two scenes bring the tang of real danger and the sweat of fear to the brow.

The stars arrive for a "replica royal film performance" of "Where No Vultures Fly", Odeon, New Street, 7th November 1951. Look away now if you want to identify them yourself! Dan Duryea, Veronica Hurst, Googie Withers, Jack Warner (partially hidden) Van Johnson, John McCallum, and Dawn Addams.

Frank O'Brien (Dame)

Patricia Grey (Principal Boy).

"SLEEPING BEAUTY", ALEXANDRA THEATRE, 1951/2

Birmingham Speedway Team, Perry Barr, 1952.

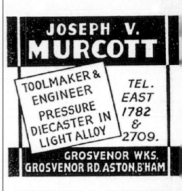
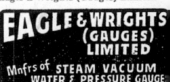

THE QUEEN FLYING HOME

The King Will Lie in State Next Week in Westminster Hall

A CHRISTIAN KING	**VALET FOUND HIM DEAD IN BED AT 7.15**
	Premier Broadcasts Tonight After Meeting Royal Party at Airport

7/2/1952

Cinemas and theatres close out of respect.

A Proclamation

to be read publicly at 11 o'clock tomorrow morning

WHEREAS it hath pleased Almighty God to call to His mercy our late Sovereign Lord King George the Sixth of blessed and glorious memory, by whose decease the Crown is solely and rightfully come to the High and Mighty Princess Elizabeth Alexandra Mary, we therefore Lords spiritual and temporal of this Realm being here assisted with these of his late Majesty's Privy Counsellors with representatives of other members of the Commonwealth with other principal gentlemen of quality with the Lord Mayor, Aldermen and Citizens of London do now hereby with one voice and consent of tongue and heart publish and proclaim the High and Mighty Princess Elizabeth Alexandra Mary is now by death of our late Sovereign of happy memory become Queen Elizabeth the Second, by the Grace of God, Queen of this Realm and all her other realms and territories, head of the Commonwealth, Defender of the Faith to whom her lieges do acknowledge all faith and constant obedience with hearty and humble affection; beseeching God by whom kings and queens do reign to bless the Royal Princess Elizabeth the Second with long and happy years to reign over us.

God Save The Queen

19

St Patrick's Day Parade, Bath Street, 16th March 1952. The Crown Inn is on the right.

Sparkhill Police Station and Library, Stratford Road, 28th May 1952.

Handsworth Park, 1952.

CADBURYS FACTORY, BOURNVILLE

ROWHEATH

PARK

KINGS NORTON

NEW RAILWAY INN

KNC.2

PERSHORE ROAD SOUTH

Yachting Pool, Bournville Lane, 1952.

The Old Dolphin Inn, Warwick Road, Acocks Green, 16th June 1952.
The publican was Alfred Lea.

Colmore Row, June1952.

The Navigation Inn, Wharf Road, Kings Norton, 1952. The publican was Ethel May Heys.

Tile Cross prefab estate, 12th August 1952. Despite their appearance they were much loved dwellings, being cool in the summer and warm in the winter.

10th Birmingham Boys' Brigade Band, Moseley Road Memorial Church, 1952.

Programme

BIRMINGHAM

BIRMINGHAM YOUTH for CHRIST

YOUTH for CHRIST

SEPTEMBER 27
PRICE SIXPENCE

An electric delivery van outside Greys, Bull Street, c 1952

Father Christmas arrives at College's (newsagents), Baldwin's Lane, Hall Green,
November 1952.

Winchurch Bros. Ltd., Sandon Road, looking towards Willow Avenue, Bearwood, 1952.

The City's newest snow plough at work in Broad Street, 15th December 1952.

Birmingham Reference Library, Ratcliff Place, 1953.

St Aidan's Church, Herbert Road, Small Heath,
8th May 1953.

Holding's Garage, Raddlebarn Road, Selly Oak, 1953.

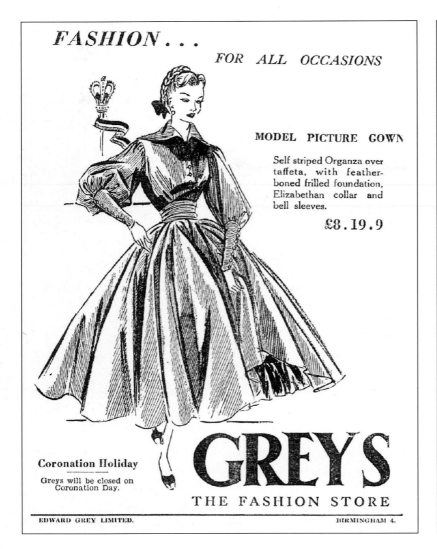

Queen Victoria's statue gets a facelift from council workers,
Victoria Square, June 1953.

The Fire Service Parade leaves the Central Fire Station to take part in the
Coronation Parade, 2nd June 1953.

Turfpits Lane Junior School Pageant, to celebrate the Coronation, June 1953.

Clearing up after the flood, Lancaster Street, 1953.

Can I interest you in an 1883 penny farthing cycle, Sir?" Mr S J Wood offers an unusual bargain, Rea Street/ Digbeth, 19th October 1953.

SMALL'S
DRAPERS

ROBIN HOOD
—— *and* ——
HALL GREEN

Lichfield Road, Aston, 1953.

Coun. L C Wheeler indicates the de-restriction sign shortly to be replaced by a 30mph sign, Bristol Road South, Northfield, 1953.

Rainbow's end

NEXT Monday will be rainbow's end for Mr. Harry Brown, who for several years has been known to thousands of Birmingham's dancers as the tall, genial manager of the West End Dance Hall.

It has always been his cherished hope that one day he might manage and keep an hotel, dispensing hospitality in the best tradition of the English inn. Next week he achieves this ambition and takes over the Rainbow Inn, Coven.

Children's Talent Night, Hippodrome, 1953.

Ventriloquist, Peter Brough, with Archie Andrews, Hippodrome, 1953.

Grange Road, with Holmwood Road on the left, Small Heath, 1953.

Warwick Road, Acocks Green, c 1953.

1954

Hubert Road, at the junction with Exeter Road, Bournbrook, 1954.

Soho Road, Handsworth, 18th January 1954.

Alcester Road South, Kings Heath, 12th April 1954.

The Three Magpies Bowling Club, off on a trip to Blackpool.
Shirley Road, Hall Green, c 1954.

Loxton Junior, Infants and Secondary Modern Schools, Loxton Street, Nechells Green, 31st May 1954.

Handsworth Park, 1954.

Gravelly Hill, Erdington, August 1954.

Grassmoor Road, Kings Norton, August 1954.

Wheelwright Road, Erdington, c 1954.

Horse Fair, with Holloway Head on the right, 1954.

Stratford Road, with Priestley Road in view, Sparkbrook, 2nd September 1954.

Bissell Street/Gooch Street, Highgate, 1954.

Newhall Street, 1954.

"Quiet Wedding", St Nicholas Amateur Dramatic Society,
Kings Norton, 21st November 1954.

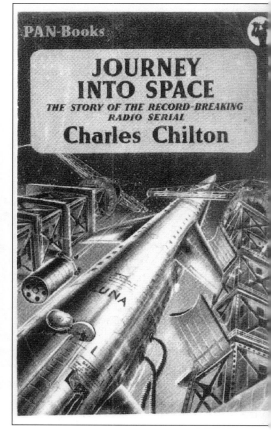

Lichfield Road/Waterworks Street, 1954.

Long Acre, Nechells, 1954.

Spencer Street (left) from Warstone Lane, with Hall Street ahead, Hockley, 1954.

1955

Frankfort Street/Gee Street, Hockley,1955.

Snow Hill, 1955.

Corporation Street, 3rd March 1955.

The Kingsway Cinema, High Street, Kings Heath, 1955. The film showing is
Elizabeth Taylor in "Elephant's Walk"

1955, April 18: The first woman freeman of Birmingham, Ald. Mrs. A. M. Howes, yesterday received a silver casket containing an illuminated copy of the City Council's resolution by which she was unanimously created a freeman.

Temple Row, 1955.

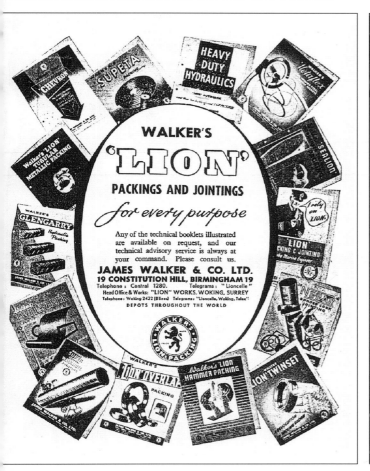
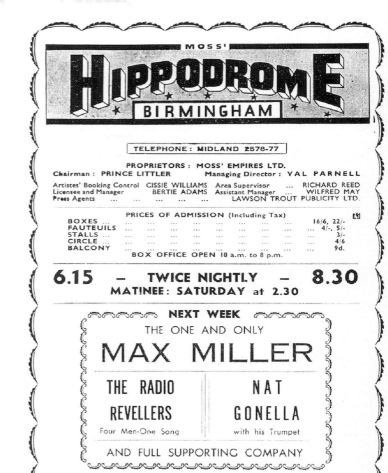

Percy Shurmer shows his obvious delight at being elected Labour MP for Sparkbrook, 27th May 1955.

"Abbotsbury Castle" arrives at Platform 7, Snow Hill Station, 30th May 1955.

Mr W H Meadows and senior managers of Dunlop Overseas Dept. with the Overseas Dept. Sports Team, which won the interdepartmental sports competition, 1955.

Hurst Street, with Smallbrook Street on the right, 15th August 1956. The site of the old Empire Theatre and later the Locarno Ballroom.

Saint James's Sunday School, Francis Street/Henry Street, 1955.

Hagley Road West, Bearwood, 10th November 1955.

A Special Constable on Point Duty, outside Freeman, Hardy & Willis Ltd., Bull Street, 1955. This is taken from where Colmore Row meets Steelhouse Lane.

Two of the city's seventy policewomen using a police telephone pillar (known as a "Blue Boy"), 1955.

Mary Malcolm.

Peter Haigh.

Sylvia Peters.

BBC TV ANNOUNCERS

Pearl Carr, Rosemary Hill, Adele Dixon and Teddy Johnson
read through Terry O'Neill's script, Alexandra Theatre,
December 1955. The pantomime was "Cinderella".

Alcester Road South, Kings Heath, 1956.

Foundations being laid on the old Big Top site,
High Street/New Street, 17th January 1956.

The distinctive tower identifies the Central Fire
Station, with the new Technical College
behind it, 1956.

Caroline Street/Regent Place, 1956.

Newton Street, 1956.

S Dibble & Son (builders) City Road, Edgbaston, 1956.

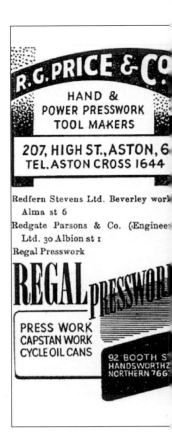

MOTOR CAR
MOTOR CYCLE R. G. KEMP SPARES &
ACCESSORIES

HAVE BLUECOL ANTI-FREEZE
PUT IN YOUR RADIATOR
WHILE YOU WAIT (5 MINS.)
No EXTRA CHARGE.

Lincoln Street, Balsall Heath, 1956.

10th Birmingham Boys' Brigade Company, 1956.

Insure with

THE
LONDON &
LANCASHIRE
INSURANCE Cº
LTD

For prospectus and
full information on
all forms of Insurance
write to:—

Midland Branch
19, BENNETT'S HILL, BIRMINGHAM, 2

Chief Administration:
7, Chancery Lane
London, W.C. 2

AUSTIN AMATEUR BOXING CLUB
BOXING
VISIT OF
BIRKENHEAD A.B.C.

TO THE
WEST
CANTEEN

AMATEUR BOXING

SATURDAY,
4th FEB.
1956
at 7.30 p.m.

AUSTIN		BIRKENHEAD
PAT O'LEARY (IRISH INTERNATIONAL)	v.	P. BRIDGES (LANCASHIRE CHAMP.)
DAN McNAMEE (SCOTTISH INTERNATIONAL)	v.	W. ROBERTS (ENGLISH INTERNATIONAL)
TONY WOODWARD (R.A.F. CHAMP.)	v.	G. MULLIN (LANCASHIRE FINALIST)
DON BURDEN	v.	W. BOYD (ARMY REP.)
JOHN HALSEY	v.	M. CAMPBELL
JOHNNY FIELD	v.	W. McATEER
JOCK WHITE	v.	R. NICHOL
GORDON STEVENS	v.	W. CHRISTIAN
RON PATTERSON	v.	A. BURNS

Also BOXING: BOB KNOWLES - MALCOLM ALLUM

TICKETS 5/- (Reserved) and 3/-
FROM USUAL SELLERS. or Mr A. C. T. CLARKE. 88 ROSELEIGH ROAD, REDNAL

Kings Norton Fellowship Basketball Team, February 1956.

Alcester Road South, Kings Heath, 1956.

Grange Road, Small Heath, 20th March 1956.

Pete Murray at a run-through of his ATV quiz show, "Hit the Limit", Aston, 1956.

Coventry Road, with Watery Lane first on the right, Bordesley, 1956.

BIRMINGHAM CITY F.C. 1955-56 SEASON

Back Row (left to right): A. LINNECOR, J. BADHAM, J. HALL, G. MERRICK, T. SMITH, LANE, R. WARHURST, K. GREEN, J. NEWMAN
Front Row (left to right): G. ASTALL, N. KINSEY, E. BROWN, Mr. A. TURNER (manager), L. BOYD (capt.), P. MURPHY, A. GOVAN, FINNEY

Maryvale Road, Bournville, 1956.

Regent Parade, 1956

The floods create havoc, Chester Road, Erdington, 3rd August 1956.

A De Havilland Rapide Bi-Plane (known as "The Dragonfly") preparing
to leave for the Isle of Wight from Elmdon Airport, 18th August 1956.

Irving Street, Edgbaston, 1956. The publican was William Dipple.

Bristol Road South, Northfield, August 1956.

St Helen's Passage, off Vittoria Street, Jewellery Quarter, 10th September 1956.

1956, September 15: Bronze statues of Watt, Boulton and Murdock, which cost £15,000, were unveiled yesterday at the Birmingham Civic Centre by Sir Percy Mills [later Lord Mills]

Northwood Street, 18th September 1956.

Smallbrook Street, with Wrottesley Street on the left, 19th September 1956.

Great Francis Street/Newdegate Street, Vauxhall, 11th December 1956.

Ladypool Road/Highgate Road, Sparkbrook, 21st December 1956.

1957

Drayton Road/Alcester Road South, Kings Heath, 1957.

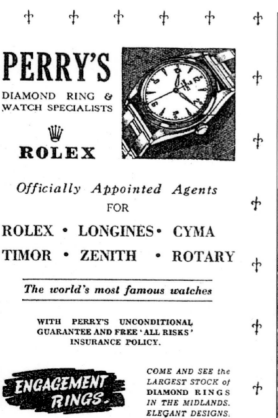

Charles Henry Street, Balsall Heath, 1957.

Fund-raising, at a Midnight Matinee for the National Federation of Boys' Clubs, involves comedian, Kenneth Horne (second left), singer, Eve Boswell and ventriloquist, Terry Hall, Alexandra Theatre, 17th February 1957.

The six top ballroom dancing couples line up to receive their prizes, 7th April 1957. The winners of the Sunday Mercury Amateur Challenge Cup were Mr and Mrs Kit Hallewell (left).

Manchester United nearly score against Aston Villa in the Cup Final, at Wembley, 4th May 1957, Villa won 2-1.

Johnny Dixon and his Villa team mates, after winning the FA Cup, 4th May 1957.

Bromford Lane, with Bromford Bridge in view, 29th July 1957. Amongst other details note the policeman on the horse on the central reservation.

Shaftmoor Lane, Acocks Green, 1957.

Looking west across the City, with Station Street on the left, 1957.

Vicarage Road, Kings Heath, 1957.

Oldfield Road, Sparkbrook, 1957.

Island Road/Holyhead Road, Handsworth, 1957.

Slade Road, Erdington, 1957.

70   Yardley Road, South Yardley, 1957.

Golden Hillock Road/Fraser Road, Sparkhill, 1957.

Great Colmore Street, 1957.

Bishopsgate Street/Broad Street, 1957.

Sampling the delights of the new Rag Market, Edgbaston Street, 20th August 1957.

College Road, Kingstanding, 1957.

Bordesley Green, with Blake Lane on the right, 8th November 1957. The Era Cinema,
which closed 15 months later, was directly opposite.

Warstone Lane, 1957.

The Harborne Picture House, Serpentine Road, 1957. It had closed in April.

CITY OF BIRMINGHAM
EDUCATION COMMITTEE

SCHOLAR'S LEAVING CERTIFICATE

THIS IS TO CERTIFY

that

Margaret Grainger

has attended

Lozells County Modern School
and is legally exempt from attendance at
School, having ceased to be of compulsory school
age as defined by Sections 35 and 38 of the
Education Act, 1944

General Remarks

*Margaret has a pleasant, friendly
disposition. She is a dependable
girl, always willing & ready to help.
Attendance & punctuality quite good*

M S Fosty
Head Teacher

E. Russell
Chief Education Officer   Date 19.12.57

Pts416

D F Tayler and Co.Ltd., (metal manufacturers)
New Hall Works, George Street, c 1957.

Frank Hawker Ltd. (electro plate and chromium plated goods mnfrs.), Spencer Street, Winson Green, 1957.

Suffolk Street/Broad Street, 1958.

Martineau Street, with Union Passage on the left, 1958.

Bull Ring, with Phillips Street on the left, 8th January 1958.

The end of the road for the Old Square Garage, Upper Priory, January 1958.

Station Road, Acocks Green, c 1958.

Thompson Passage, 1958. Just off the Bull Ring.

BOURNVILLE FILM SOCIETY
Twelfth Season — 1957-58
TUESDAY, 18th FEBRUARY, at 7.15 p.m.
CONCERT HALL, BOURNVILLE

Ninety-fourth Programme

The Committee thanks all those members who returned the questionnaire last year's programme and, feeling that they would be interested in the results, expects to give a brief synopsis next month.

———oOo———

As you know, films are often withdrawn from circulation for various reasons—the owner may decide that there is no more financial profit in the film and destroy the negative, or he may sell the copyright for remake on television here or in the United States. All this means that important and irreplaceable films are being lost, and although the British Film Institute tries to obtain a copy of films before they are destroyed, this is not always possible. You will probably be appalled by the list of films now withdrawn from film society (or any other) circulation:—

Things to Come.	Belle et la Bête.
Waterloo Bridge.	Jour de Fête.
Four Feathers.	Visiteurs du Soir.
Escape to Happiness.	Shoeshine.
Tawny Pippett.	Bank Holiday.
Magnificent Ambersons.	Blue Angel.
How Green was my Valley.	Way Ahead.
Gone with the Wind.	Next of Kin.
Forever and a Day.	Quai des Orfèvres.
Orphée.	Un Carnet du Bal.
Lady Vanishes (35 mm.).	Pépé le Moko.
Hellzapoppin (June 1958).	Day at the Races (35 mm.).
Sang d'un Poete (35 mm.).	The Great Dictator.
Marius Trilogy.	Greed.
Citizen Kane.	Open City.

The second list gives films which are printed on nitrate stocks only, and for that reason cannot be shown in the Concert Hall, Bournville. Again these are interesting films which we here cannot screen because of the bye-laws which insist on the use of safety stock prints at public film shows:—

The Third Man.	Overlanders.
Grapes of Wrath.	Matter of Life and Death.
Letter from an Unknown Woman.	Ivan the Terrible.
Brief Encounter.	Enfants du Paradis.
Dead of Night.	Emperor's Nightingale.
Tales of Hoffman.	

———oOo———

Tonight's Programme

MUSIC BOX   **U.S.A. 1932—30 mins.**

This early Laurel and Hardy film, well worn but still wearing well, describes the delivery of a pianola by the two comics, who are in the haulage business (in a very small way, of course). The destination turns out to be a house at the top of an extremely long and fairly steep flight of steps, with an ornamental pond at the top. Need we say more? The humour is rather unsubtle, but the facial expressions of both men are a joy to watch.

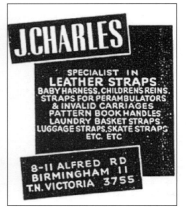

Coventry Road/Bowyer Street, Bordesley, 1958.

British Timken Co.Ltd., (tapered roller bearings), Cheston Road, Aston, 1958.

Bandleader, Ken Mackintosh, compares shoe sizes with American singer, Johnnie Ray, Town Hall 16th April 1958.

Our own Anne Heywood and American star, Howard Keel in the all-action film, "Floods Of Fear", 1958.

Singing stars, The Kaye Sisters, meet the Lord Mayor and Lady Mayoress, Ald. and Mrs J J Grogan, ABC TV's Alpha Studios, Aston, 21st April 1958.

Soho Guest House, Soho Road/Rose Hill Road, Handsworth, 1958.

Birmingham Liberal municipal election candidates plan their campaign for the May elections, 29th April 1958.

Bradford Street, 7th May 1958.

Dale End, from Coleshill Street, 1958.

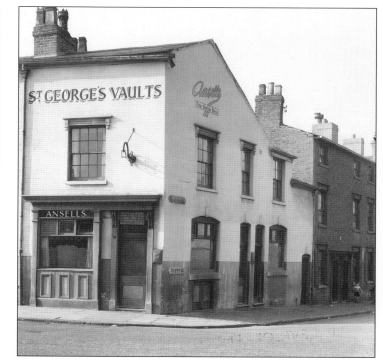

Great Hampton Row/Unett Street, 1958.

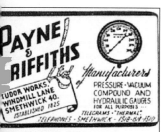

Pershore Road, Stirchley, 23rd May 1958.

Warwick Road, with Lincoln Road in the centre, Acocks Green, 1958.

Park Hill Road, Harborne, 1958.

Poplar Road, Sparkhill, 1958.

Yardley Fields Road/Lyttleton Road, Stechford, 1958.

Woodthorpe Road/Alcester Road South, Kings Heath, 1958.

Comedian, Michael Bentine, rehearses with Shirley Bassey (his guest singer) for his series, "After Hours", Alpha Studios, Aston, 1958.

Duke Ellington, the Odeon, New Street, October 1958.

Tea break at the Alpha Studios, 16th November 1958.

Rehearsal time for "Bid For Fame", Alpha Studios, 16th November 1958.

Noele Gordon, surrounded by technical crews from various departments, Alpha Studios, Aston, c 1958.

The control room at Alpha Studios, with the face of continuity man, McDonald Hobley, on the screen, 16th November 1958.

Members of the Modernaires ready for action at the
Ritz Ballroom, Bordesley Green, 1958.

Singer, David Whitfield, gets to grips with Hermene French and Ron Parry,
"Robinson Crusoe", Hippodrome, 23rd December 1958.

Bull Street, 1959.

Count Basie brings his orchestra to the Odeon,
New Street, 17th February 1959.

Louis Armstrong, appearing with his All-Stars,
Odeon, 5th March 1959.

Watford Road, Cotteridge, 1959.

The Winson Green Picture House, Winson Green Road/
Wellington Road, 19th March 1959. Mr A W Hall,
the Manager, is on the left.

The last film ready to be shown, Winson Green
Picture House, 21st March 1959. The film was
"Sea of Sand", starring Richard Attenborough.

The Globe, Vauxhall Road, 1959.

Waldorf Café, Walford Road, Sparkbrook, 1959.

Demolition time in Temple Row, March 1959. The Great Western Arcade can be seen on the left.

Navigation Street, 1959.

Treasure Trove, Pershore Road, Cotteridge, 19th April 1959.

Edgbaston Road, Balsall Heath, 1959.

The Couriers rehearsing, minus vocalist Phil King, Bushmore Hall, Cresswell Road, Hall Green, 1959.

American singer, Billy Eckstine, appearing in variety at the Hippodrome, 24th-29th August 1959.

High Street, Deritend, 1959.

George "The Casual Comedian" Martin appears in "Cinderella", Alexandra Theatre, December 1959.

Edmundo Ros, with his Latin-American Orchestra, appears on BBC TV, December 1959.

Monument Road, with Ledsam Street on the right, Ladywood, 1959.

Monument Road, Ladywood, 30th December 1959.

Back Cover: Aston Hippodrome, 11th February 1958.

ACKNOWLEDGEMENTS

(for providing photographs, encouragement and numerous other favours)

Keith Ackrill; Peter Ashlington; The Birmingham City Council Dept. of Planning and Architecture; The Birmingham Post and Mail Ltd.; Beryl Brittain; Arthur Brown; John and Maisie Brown; The Late Arthur Camwell; Dave Carpenter; Wilf Clare; Roy Dillon; Paula Earle; Tony Eaton; Ray Green; Joyce Hargreaves; Phil Haycock; The Heartlands Local History Society; John Hill; Royston Kemp; Eddie Large; Dennis Moore; Gertrude and Alan Peters; Brian Pinkerton; Douglas Price; Dave Robinson; Geoffrey Round; Jean Russell; Sheila Seabourne; Keith Shakespeare; Roger Smith; Len Thompson; Michael Vincent; Joan Ward; Rosemary Wilkes; Anne Williams; Keith Williams; Ken Windsor.

Please forgive any possible omissions. Every effort has been made to include all organisations and individuals involved in the book.

Booking in advance for holiday trains, Snow Hill Station, c 1959.